LIFT UP YOUR HEARTS

Music for the Order of Mass According to the Third Edition of the Roman Missal

LITURGICAL PRESS
Collegeville, Minnesota

www.litpress.org

Cover design by Ann Blattner. Art by Martin Erspamer, OSB, a monk of Saint Meinrad Archabbey.

Published with the approval of the
Committee on Divine Worship
United States Conference of Catholic Bishops

Excerpts from the English translation and chants of *The Roman Missal* © 2010, International Commission on English in the Liturgy Corporation (ICEL); the English translation of the Lenten Gospel Acclamations from *Lectionary for Mass* © 1969, 1981, 1997, ICEL. All rights reserved.

ISBN 978-0-8146-3379-3

Contents

THE ORDER OF MASS

THE INTRODUCTORY RITES

When the Entrance Chant has concluded, the Priest and the faithful sign themselves with the Sign of the Cross. The Priest sings or says:

In the name of the Father, and of the Son,
and of the Holy Spirit.

The people reply:

A - men.   A - men.

Then the Priest greets the people:

1. The grace of our Lord Jesus Christ,
   and the love of God,
   and the communion of the Holy Spirit
   be with you all.

2. Grace to you and peace from God our Father
   and the Lord Jesus Christ.

3. The Lord be with you.

   In this first greeting, a Bishop sings or says:
   Peace be with you.

The people reply:

And with your spir - it.   And with your spir-it.

The Priest, or a Deacon, or another minister, may very briefly introduce the faithful to the Mass of the day.

PENITENTIAL ACT

The Priest invites the faithful, saying:

> Brethren (brothers and sisters), let us acknowledge
>   our sins,
> and so prepare ourselves to celebrate the sacred
>   mysteries.

A brief pause for silence follows.

Then one of the following formula of general confession is used:

1 **I confess to almighty God
and to you, my brothers and sisters,
that I have greatly sinned,
in my thoughts and in my words,
in what I have done and in what I have
    failed to do,**

And, striking their breast, they say:

**through my fault, through my fault,
through my most grievous fault;
therefore I ask blessed Mary ever-Virgin,
all the Angels and Saints,
and you, my brothers and sisters,
to pray for me to the Lord our God.**

2 *The Priest then sings or says:*

> Have mercy on us, O Lord.

The people reply:

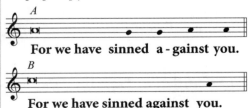

A

For we have sinned a - gainst you.

B

For we have sinned against you.

The Priest:

Show us, O Lord, your mercy.

The people reply:

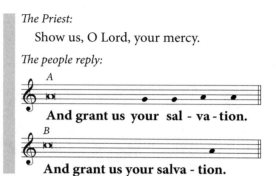

And grant us your sal - va - tion.

And grant us your salva - tion.

3. *The Priest, or a Deacon, or another minister, then sings or says the invocations, followed by Kyrie, eleison (Lord, have mercy). The people repeat the response:*

Lord, have mer - cy. Kýrie, e - lé - i - son.
Christ, have mer - cy. Christe, e - lé - i - son.
Lord, have mer - cy. Kýrie, e - lé - i - son.

Lord, have mer - cy. Kýrie, elé - ison.
Christ, have mer - cy. Christe, elé - ison.
Lord, have mer - cy. Kýrie, elé - ison.

The absolution by the Priest follows:

May almighty God have mercy on us,
forgive us our sins,
and bring us to everlasting life.

The people reply:

A - men. A - men.

KYRIE

The Kyrie eleison (Lord, have mercy) *invocations follow, unless they have just occurred in a formula of the Penitential Act. The people repeat the invocation after the Priest or Deacon.*

Kyrie, eleison.	*or*	**Lord, have mercy.**
Christe, eleison.	*or*	**Christ, have mercy.**
Kyrie, eleison.	*or*	**Lord, have mercy.**

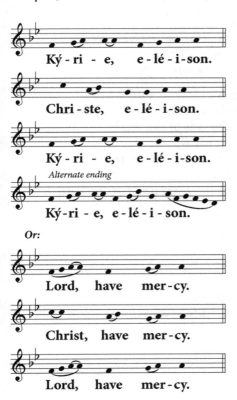

Ký - ri - e,   e - lé - i - son.

Chri - ste,   e - lé - i - son.

Ký - ri - e,   e - lé - i - son.

Alternate ending

Ký - ri - e, e - lé - i - son.

Or:

Lord,   have   mer - cy.

Christ,   have   mer - cy.

Lord,   have   mer - cy.

GLORIA

When it is prescribed, this hymn is either said or sung:

**Glory to God in the highest,
and on earth peace to people of good will.**

**We praise you,
we bless you,
we adore you,
we glorify you,
we give you thanks for your great glory,
Lord God, heavenly King,
O God, almighty Father.**

**Lord Jesus Christ, Only Begotten Son,
Lord God, Lamb of God, Son of the Father,
you take away the sins of the world,
    have mercy on us;
you take away the sins of the world,
    receive our prayer;
you are seated at the right hand of the Father,
    have mercy on us.**

**For you alone are the Holy One,
you alone are the Lord,
you alone are the Most High,
Jesus Christ,
with the Holy Spirit,
in the glory of God the Father.**

Amen.

Glo-ry to God in the high-est,

and on earth peace to peo-ple of good will.

We praise you, we bless you, we a-dore you,

we glo-ri-fy you, we give you thanks

for your great glo-ry, Lord God, heav-en-

ly King, O God, al-might-y Fa-ther.

Lord Je-sus Christ, On-ly Be-got-ten Son,

Lord God, Lamb of God, Son of the Fa-ther,

you take a-way the sins of the world,

have mer-cy on us; you take a-way the

sins of the world, re-ceive our prayer;

you are seat-ed at the right hand of the Fa-ther, have mer-cy on us. For you a-lone are the Ho-ly One, you a-lone are the Lord, you a-lone are the Most High, Je-sus Christ, with the Ho-ly Spir-it, in the glo-ry of God the Fa - ther. A - men.

COLLECT

When the Gloria has concluded, the Priest sings or says:

Let us pray.

All pray in silence. Then the Priest sings or says the Collect prayer and the people reply:

A - men.   A - men.

All are seated.

THE LITURGY OF THE WORD

FIRST READING

At the conclusion of the reading, the reader sings or says:

The word of the Lord.

The people reply:

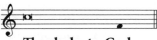

Thanks be to God.

RESPONSORIAL PSALM

The psalmist or cantor sings or says the Psalm, with the people making the response.

SECOND READING

At the conclusion of the reading, the reader sings or says:

The word of the Lord.

The people reply:

Thanks be to God.

ACCLAMATION BEFORE THE GOSPEL

All stand.

Al-le-lu-ia,   al - le-lu-ia,   al - le - lu - ia.

During Lent, one of the following acclamations may be used:

Praise to you, Lord Jesus Christ, King of endless glory!
Praise and honor to you, Lord Jesus Christ!
Glory and praise to you, Lord Jesus Christ!
Glory to you, Word of God, Lord Jesus Christ!

GOSPEL

The Deacon, or the Priest, then proceeds to the ambo to read the Gospel. Once at the ambo he sings or says:

The Lord be with you.

The people reply:

And with your spir-it.   And with your spir-it.

The Deacon, or the Priest:

A reading from the holy Gospel according to *N.*

The people reply:

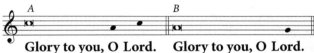

Glory to you, O Lord.   Glory to you, O Lord.

At the end of the Gospel, the Deacon, or the Priest, sings or says:

The Gospel of the Lord.

The people reply:

Praise to you, Lord Je-sus Christ.

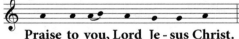

Praise to you, Lord Je-sus Christ.

All are seated.

HOMILY

PROFESSION OF FAITH

At the end of the homily, the Symbol or Profession of Faith or Creed, when prescribed, is either said or sung. All stand.

NICENE CREED

I believe in one God,
the Father almighty,
maker of heaven and earth,
of all things visible and invisible.

I believe in one Lord Jesus Christ,
the Only Begotten Son of God,
born of the Father before all ages.
God from God, Light from Light,
true God from true God,
begotten, not made, consubstantial with the Father;
through him all things were made.
For us men and for our salvation
he came down from heaven,

At the words that follow, up to and including and became man, *all bow.*

and by the Holy Spirit was incarnate
   of the Virgin Mary,
and became man.

For our sake he was crucified under Pontius Pilate,
he suffered death and was buried,
and rose again on the third day
in accordance with the Scriptures.
He ascended into heaven
and is seated at the right hand of the Father.
He will come again in glory
to judge the living and the dead
and his kingdom will have no end.

I believe in the Holy Spirit, the Lord, the giver of life,
who proceeds from the Father and the Son,
who with the Father and the Son is adored and
   glorified,
who has spoken through the prophets.

I believe in one, holy, catholic and apostolic Church.
I confess one Baptism for the forgiveness of sins
and I look forward to the resurrection of the dead
and the life of the world to come. Amen.

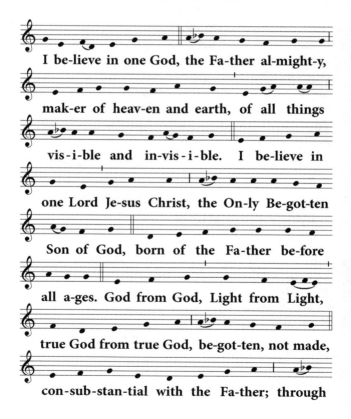

I be-lieve in one God, the Fa-ther al-might-y,

mak-er of heav-en and earth, of all things

vis-i-ble and in-vis-i-ble. I be-lieve in

one Lord Je-sus Christ, the On-ly Be-got-ten

Son of God, born of the Fa-ther be-fore

all a-ges. God from God, Light from Light,

true God from true God, be-got-ten, not made,

con-sub-stan-tial with the Fa-ther; through

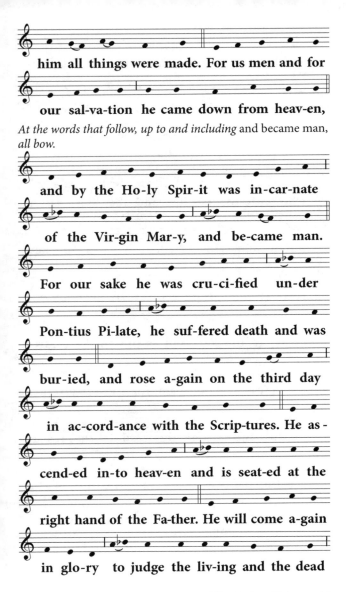

him all things were made. For us men and for

our sal-va-tion he came down from heav-en,

At the words that follow, up to and including and became man,
all bow.

and by the Ho-ly Spir-it was in-car-nate

of the Vir-gin Mar-y, and be-came man.

For our sake he was cru-ci-fied   un-der

Pon-tius Pi-late, he suf-fered death and was

bur-ied, and rose a-gain on the third day

in ac-cord-ance with the Scrip-tures. He as -

cend-ed in-to heav-en and is seat-ed at the

right hand of the Fa-ther. He will come a-gain

in glo-ry   to judge the liv-ing and the dead

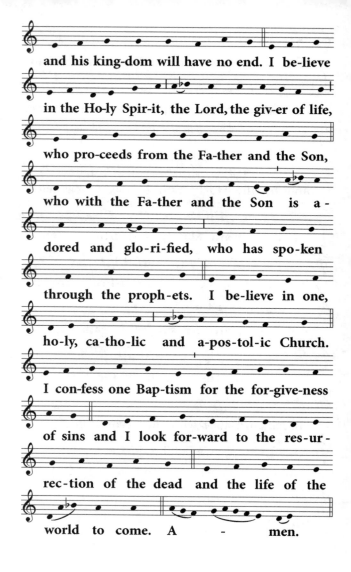

and his king-dom will have no end. I be-lieve

in the Ho-ly Spir-it, the Lord, the giv-er of life,

who pro-ceeds from the Fa-ther and the Son,

who with the Fa-ther and the Son is a -

dored and glo-ri-fied, who has spo-ken

through the proph-ets. I be-lieve in one,

ho-ly, ca-tho-lic and a-pos-tol-ic Church.

I con-fess one Bap-tism for the for-give-ness

of sins and I look for-ward to the res-ur -

rec-tion of the dead and the life of the

world to come. A - men.

APOSTLES' CREED

Instead of the Niceno-Constantinopolitan Creed, especially during Lent and Easter Time, the baptismal Symbol of the Roman Church, known as the Apostles' Creed, may be used.

I believe in God,
the Father almighty,
Creator of heaven and earth,
and in Jesus Christ, his only Son, our Lord,

At the words that follow, up to and including the Virgin Mary, *all bow.*

who was conceived by the Holy Spirit,
born of the Virgin Mary,
suffered under Pontius Pilate,
was crucified, died and was buried;
he descended into hell;
on the third day he rose again from the dead;
he ascended into heaven,
and is seated at the right hand of
God the Father almighty;
from there he will come to judge the living
and the dead.

I believe in the Holy Spirit,
the holy catholic Church,
the communion of saints,
the forgiveness of sins,
the resurrection of the body,
and life everlasting. Amen.

UNIVERSAL PRAYER

Then follows the Prayer of the Faithful or Bidding Prayers. The deacon or another minister sings or says the invocations and the people make the response according to local custom.

1 Lord, we ask you, hear our prayer.

2 Hear us, O Christ.

3 Lord, hear our prayer.

4 Lord, have mer - cy.

5 Lord, hear our prayer.

6 Ký - ri - e, e - lé - i - son.

After the concluding prayer, the people reply:

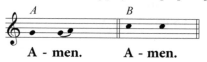

A A - men. **B** A - men.

All are seated.

THE LITURGY OF THE EUCHARIST

While the gifts of bread and wine are brought forward, placed on the altar and prepared, a hymn may be sung. If there is no singing, the Priest may pray the prayers aloud, to which the people reply:

Blessed be God for ever.

The Priest continues:

Pray, brethren (brothers and sisters),
that my sacrifice and yours
may be acceptable to God,
the almighty Father.

The people stand and reply:

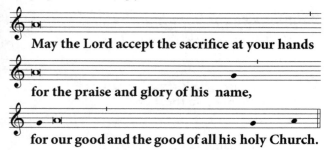

May the Lord accept the sacrifice at your hands

for the praise and glory of his name,

for our good and the good of all his holy Church.

The Priest sings or says the Prayer over the Offerings and the people reply:

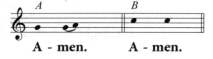

A - men.   A - men.

THE EUCHARISTIC PRAYER

Then the Priest begins the Eucharistic Prayer:

The Lord be with you.

The people reply:

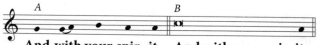

And with your spir-it.   And with your spir-it.

The Priest:

Lift up your hearts.

The people reply:

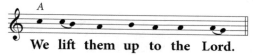

We lift them up to the Lord.

We lift them up to the Lord.

The Priest:

Let us give thanks to the Lord our God.

The people reply:

It is right and just.   It is right and just.

The Priest continues with the Preface.

SANCTUS

At the end of the Preface, all sing or say together the Sanctus:

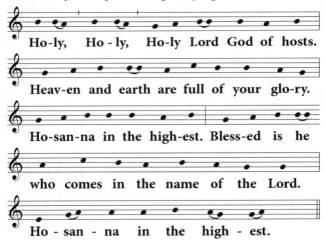

Ho-ly, Ho-ly, Ho-ly Lord God of hosts.

Heav-en and earth are full of your glo-ry.

Ho-san-na in the high-est. Bless-ed is he

who comes in the name of the Lord.

Ho - san - na in the high - est.

All kneel. The Priest then continues with one of the Eucharistic Prayers.

MYSTERIUM FIDEI

After the words of Institution, the Priest sings or says:

The mystery of faith.

The people reply:

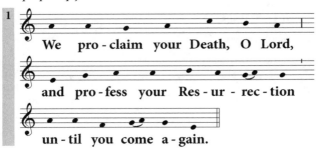

We pro - claim your Death, O Lord,

and pro - fess your Res - ur - rec - tion

un - til you come a - gain.

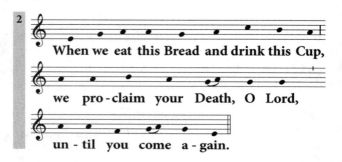

2

When we eat this Bread and drink this Cup,

we pro-claim your Death, O Lord,

un-til you come a-gain.

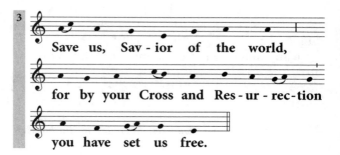

3

Save us, Sav-ior of the world,

for by your Cross and Res-ur-rec-tion

you have set us free.

The Priest concludes the Eucharistic Prayer by singing or saying the Doxology:

Through him, and with him, and in him,
O God, almighty Father,
in the unity of the Holy Spirit,
all glory and honor is yours,
for ever and ever.

The people reply:

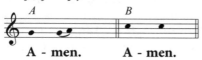

A B

A - men.   A - men.

All stand.

THE COMMUNION RITE

LORD'S PRAYER

The Priest invites all to pray the Lord's Prayer.

Our Fa-ther, who art in heav-en, hal-lowed
be thy name; thy king-dom come, thy will
be done on earth as it is in heav-en.
Give us this day our dai-ly bread, and forgive us our tres-pass-es, as we for-give those
who tres-pass a-gainst us; and lead us not into temp-ta-tion, but de-liv-er us from e-vil.

The Priest continues:

Deliver us, Lord . . . of our Savior, Jesus Christ.

The people reply:

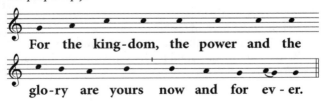

For the king-dom, the power and the
glo-ry are yours now and for ev-er.

SIGN OF PEACE

The Priest sings or says the prayer and the people reply:

A - men.   A - men.

The Priest:

> The peace of the Lord be with you always.

The people reply:

And with your spir - it.   And with your spir-it.

The people exchange a sign of peace according to local custom.

AGNUS DEI

Lamb of God, you take a - way the sins

of the world, have mer-cy on us.

of the world, grant us peace.

Then the Priest sings or says:

> Behold the Lamb of God,
> behold him who takes away the sins of the world.
> Blessed are those called to the supper of the Lamb.

The Priest and the people together sing or say:

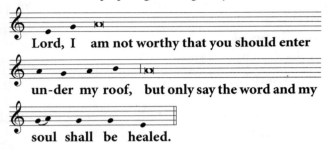

Lord, I am not worthy that you should enter un-der my roof, but only say the word and my soul shall be healed.

RECEPTION OF HOLY COMMUNION

The Priest or minister raises a host (or a chalice) slightly and shows it to each communicant, saying:

The Body of Christ. *or* The Blood of Christ.

The communicant replies:

Amen.

PRAYER AFTER COMMUNION

All stand and the Priest sings or says:

Let us pray.

All pray in silence with the Priest for a while, unless silence has just been observed. Then the Priest sings or says the Prayer and the people reply:

A - men.   A - men.

THE CONCLUDING RITES

GREETING

The Priest sings or says:

The Lord be with you.

The people reply:

And with your spir - it.   And with your spir-it.

When a Bishop greets the people, he continues:

Blessed be the name of the Lord.

The people reply:

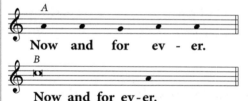

Now   and   for   ev - er.

Now   and   for   ev-er.

The Bishop:

Our help is in the name of the Lord.

The people reply:

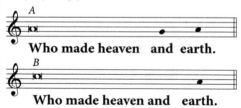

Who made heaven   and   earth.

Who made heaven and   earth.

BLESSING

The Priest blesses the people, singing or saying:

May almighty God bless you,
the Father, and the Son, ✚ and the Holy Spirit.

The people reply:

A - men.   A - men.

The above blessing may be preceded by another more solemn blessing or by a prayer over the people.

DISMISSAL

The Deacon, or Priest, dismisses the people, singing or saying:

1 Go forth, the Mass is ended.

2 Go and announce the Gospel of the Lord.

3 Go in peace, glorifying the Lord by your life.

4 Go in peace.

The people reply:

Thanks be to God.   Thanks be to God.

During the Easter season, the people reply:

Thanks be to God, al-le-lu-ia, al-le - lu - ia.

Mass I—The Psallite Mass:
At the Table of the Lord

by The Collegeville Composers Group

1. Kyrie I

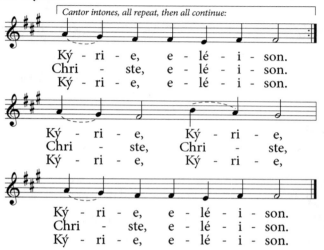

Cantor intones, all repeat, then all continue:

Ký - ri - e,	e - lé - i - son.
Chri - ste,	e - lé - i - son.
Ký - ri - e,	e - lé - i - son.

Ký - ri - e,	Ký - ri - e,
Chri - ste,	Chri - ste,
Ký - ri - e,	Ký - ri - e,

Ký - ri - e,	e - lé - i - son.
Chri - ste,	e - lé - i - son.
Ký - ri - e,	e - lé - i - son.

2. Kyrie II

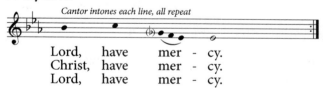

Cantor intones each line, all repeat

Lord,	have	mer - cy.
Christ,	have	mer - cy.
Lord,	have	mer - cy.

3. Gloria (English)

1. Glory to God in the highest,
2. We praise you, we bless you, we a - dore you,
3. Lord God, heavenly King,

1. and on earth peace to people of good will.
2. we glorify you,
   we give you thanks for } your great glory,
3. O God, al - might - y Father.

4. Lord Jesus Christ, Only Be - got - ten Son,
5. you take away the sins of the world,
6. you take away the sins of the world,
7. you are seated at the right hand of the Father,

4. Lord God, Lamb of God, Son of the Father,
5. have mercy on us;
6. receive our prayer;
7. have mercy on us.

8. For you a - lone are the Holy One,
9. you alone are
   the Most High, } Jesus Christ,
10. A - men,

8. you alone are the Lord,
9. with the Holy Spirit,}
   in the glory of } God the Father.
10. A - men.

Text: *The Roman Missal*, © 2010, ICEL. All rights reserved.
Music: *Psallite Mass: At the Table of the Lord*, The Collegeville Composers Group, © 2010.
Published and administered by Liturgical Press, Collegeville, MN 56321. All rights reserved.

4. Gloria (Spanish)

1. Gloria a Dios en el cielo,
2. Por tu inmensa gloria te ala - bamos,
3. te glorifi - camos,
4. Señor Dios, Rey celes - tial,

1. y en la tierra paz a los hombres que ama ⎱ el Se - ñor.
2. te bendecimos, te a - do - ramos,
3. te da - mos gracias,
4. Dios Padre todo - po - de - roso.

5. Señor, Hijo único Je - su - cristo.
6. tú que quitas el peca - do del mundo,
7. tú que quitas el peca - do del mundo,
8. tú que estás sentado a la dere - cha del Padre,

5. Señor Dios, Cordero de Dios, Hijo del Padre;
6. ten piedad de nos - otros;
7. atiende nue - stra súplica;
8. ten piedad de nos - otros;

9. porque sólo tú eres Santo,
10. sólo tú Al - tísimo, Jesu - cristo,
11. A - men,

9. sólo tú Se - ñor,
10. con el Espíritu Santo en la gloria de Dios Padre.
11. A - mén.

Text: *Misal Romano*, © 1999, 2002, Obra Nacional de la Buena Prensa, A.C. All rights reserved.
Music: *Psallite Mass: At the Table of the Lord*, The Collegeville Composers Group, © 2010.
Published and administered by Liturgical Press, Collegeville, MN 56321. All rights reserved.

5. Gloria (Latin)

1. Glória in ex - célsis Deo
2. Laudámus te, bene - dícimus te,
3. grátias ágimus tibi
4. Dómine Deus, Rex cæ - léstis,

1. et in terra pax homínibus bonæ vo-lun - tátis.
2. adorámus te, glo - ri - fi-cámus te,
3. propter magnam gló - ri-am tuam,
4. Deus Pa - ter om-nípotens.

5. Dómine Fili Unigénite, Ie - su Christe,
6. qui tollis pec - cá - ta mundi,
7. qui tollis pec - cá - ta mundi,
8. Qui sedes ad déx - te - ram Patris,

5. Dómine Deus, Agnus Dei, Fíli - us Patris,
6. miseré - re nobis;
7. súscipe deprecatió - nem nostram.
8. miseré - re nobis.

9. Quóniam tu solus Sanctus,
10. tu solus Altíssimus, Iesu Christe,
11. A - men,

9. tu so-lus Dóminus,
10. cum Sancto Spíritu: in glória De - i Patris.
11. A - men.

Text: *Missale Romanum.*

Music: *Psallite Mass: At the Table of the Lord,* The Collegeville Composers Group, © 2010.
Published and administered by Liturgical Press, Collegeville, MN 56321. All rights reserved.

6. Gospel Acclamation

All:
Al-le-lu-ia, al-le - lu - ia.

Cantor:

All:
Al-le-lu-ia, al-le - lu - ia.

Cantor:

All:
Al-le-lu-ia, al-le - lu - ia.

7. Gospel Acclamation (Lent)

Refrain

Cantor:
Glo-ry to you. . .

All:
Glo-ry to you,—— glo-ry to you,——

glo - ry and praise to you.——

Verse

Cantor: *All:*
. . .glo-ry and praise to you.——

Cantor: *All:*
. . .glo-ry and praise to you.——

8. Gospel Acclamation (Easter)

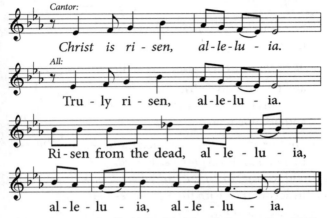

Cantor:
Christ is ri - sen, al-le-lu - ia.

All:
Tru - ly ri - sen, al-le-lu - ia.

Ri - sen from the dead, al - le - lu - ia,

al - le - lu - ia, al - le - lu - ia.

9. Nicene Creed (English)

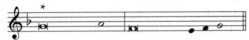

* I believe in one <u>God</u>,
  the Fa-<u>ther</u> almighty,
* maker of heaven and <u>earth</u>,
  of all things visible <u>and</u> invisible.
* I believe in one Lord Jesus Christ,
  the Only Begotten Son of <u>God</u>,
  born of the Father be-<u>fore</u> all ages.
* God from God, Light from <u>Light</u>,
  true <u>God</u> from true God,
* begotten, not <u>made</u>,
  consubstantial with the Father;
  through him all <u>things</u> were made.

* For us men and for our sal-<u>va</u>tion
  he came <u>down</u> from heaven,

  All bow from here through the words and became man.

* and by the Holy Spirit
  was incarnate of the Virgin <u>Ma</u>ry,
  and <u>be</u>came man.

* For our sake he was crucified under Pontius <u>Pi</u>late,
  he suffered death <u>and</u> was buried,

* and rose again on the <u>third</u> day
  in accordance <u>with</u> the Scriptures.

* He ascended into <u>hea</u>ven
  and is seated at the right hand <u>of</u> the Father.

* He will come again in glory
  to judge the living and the <u>dead</u>
  and his kingdom will <u>have</u> no end.

* I believe in the Holy Spirit, the Lord, the giver of <u>life</u>,
  who proceeds from the Father <u>and</u> the Son,

* who with the Father and the Son is adored and <u>glo</u>rified,
  who has spoken <u>through</u> the prophets.

* I believe in one, holy, <u>ca</u>tholic
  and apo-<u>sto</u>lic Church.

* I confess one <u>Bap</u>tism
  for the forgive-<u>ness</u> of sins

* and I look forward to the resurrection of the <u>dead</u>
  and the life of the world to <u>come</u>. Amen.

Text: *The Roman Missal,* © 2010, ICEL. All rights reserved.
Music: *Psallite Mass: At the Table of the Lord,* The Collegeville Composers Group, © 2010.
Published and administered by Liturgical Press, Collegeville, MN 56321. All rights reserved.

10. Nicene Creed (Spanish)

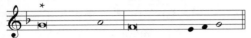

* Creo en un solo <u>Dios</u>,
  Padre todo-po<u>de</u>roso,
* Creador del cielo y de la <u>tie</u>rra,
  de todo lo visible y lo in<u>vi</u>sible.
* Creo en un solo Señor, Jesucristo,
      Hijo único de <u>Dios</u>,
  nacido del Padre antes de to-<u>dos</u> los siglos:
* Dios de Dios, Luz de <u>Luz</u>,
  Dios verdadero de Dios <u>ver</u>dadero,
* engendrado, no cre-<u>a</u>do,
  de la misma naturaleza del Padre,
      por quien to-<u>do</u> fue hecho;
* que por nosotros, los hombres,
      y por nuestra salva-<u>ción</u>
  ba-<u>jó</u> del cielo,

En las palabras que siguen, hasta se hizo hombre, *todos se inclinan.*

* y por obra del Espíritu Santo
      se encarnó de María, la <u>Vir</u>gen,
  y se <u>hi</u>zo hombre;

* y por nuestra causa fue crucificado
      en tiempos de Poncio Pi-<u>la</u>to,
  padeció y fue <u>se</u>pultado,
* y resucitó al tercer <u>dí</u>a,
  según las <u>E</u>scrituras,
* y subió al <u>cie</u>lo,
  y está sentado a la dere-<u>cha</u> del Padre;
* y de nuevo vendrá con gloria
      para juzgar a vivos y <u>muer</u>tos,
  y su reino no <u>ten</u>drá fin.

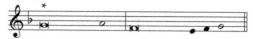

* Creo en el Espíritu Santo, Señor y dador de <u>vi</u>da,
  que procede del Padre <u>y</u> del Hijo,
* que con el Padre y el Hijo
          recibe una misma adoración y <u>glo</u>ria,
  y que habló por <u>los</u> profetas.
* Creo en la I-<u>gle</u>sia,
  que es una, santa, católica y <u>a</u>postólica.
* Confieso que hay un solo bau-<u>tis</u>mo
  para el perdón de <u>los</u> pecados.
* Espero la resurrección de los <u>muer</u>tos
  y la vida del mundo futu-<u>ro</u>. Amén.

11. Nicene Creed (Latin)

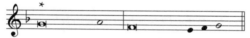

* Credo in unum <u>De</u>um,
  Patrem om-<u>ni</u>poténtem,
* factórem cæli et <u>ter</u>ræ,
  visibílium ómnium et in-<u>vi</u>sibílium.
* Et in unum Dóminum Iesum Christum,
          Fílium Dei Uni-<u>gé</u>nitum,
  et ex Patre natum ante óm-<u>ni</u>a sǽcula.
* Deum de Deo, lumen de <u>lú</u>mine,
  Deum verum de <u>De</u>o vero,
* génitum, non <u>fac</u>tum,
  consubstantiálem Patri: per quem ómnia <u>fac</u>ta sunt.

* Qui propter nos hómines et propter nostram sa-<u>lú</u>tem
descén-<u>dit</u> de cælis.

Ad verba quæ sequuntur, usque ad factus est, *omnes se inclinant.*

* Et incarnátus est de Spíritu Sancto ex María <u>Vír</u>gine,
et homo <u>fa</u>ctus est.

* Crucifíxus étiam pro nobis sub Póntio Pi-<u>lá</u>to;
passus <u>et</u> sepúltus est,
* et resurréxit tértia <u>die</u>,
secún-<u>dum</u> Scriptúras,
* et ascéndit in <u>cæ</u>lum,
sedet ad déx-<u>te</u>ram Patris.
* Et íterum ventúrus est cum glória,
iudicáre vivos et <u>mór</u>tuos,
cuius regni non <u>e</u>rit finis.
* Et in Spíritum Sanctum, Dóminum et vivifi-<u>cán</u>tem:
qui ex Patre Filió-<u>que</u> procédit.
* Qui cum Patre et Fílio simul adorátur
et conglorifi-<u>cá</u>tur:
qui locútus est <u>per</u> prophétas.
* Et unam, sanctam, ca-<u>thó</u>licam
et apostóli-<u>cam</u> Ecclésiam.
* Confíteor unum bap-<u>tís</u>ma
in remissiónem <u>pec</u>catórum.
* Et exspécto resurrectiónem mortu-<u>ó</u>rum,
et vitam ventúri sǽcu-<u>li</u>. Amen.

Text: *Missale Romanum.*
Music: *Psallite Mass: At the Table of the Lord,* The Collegeville Composers Group, © 2010.
Published and administered by Liturgical Press, Collegeville, MN 56321. All rights reserved.

12. Apostles' Creed (English)

* I believe in God, the Father al-<u>might</u>y,
    Creator of hea-<u>ven</u> and earth,
* and in Jesus Christ, his only Son, our <u>Lord</u>,

All bow from here through the words born of the Virgin Mary.

  who was conceived by the Holy Spirit,
       born of the <u>Vir</u>gin Mary,

* suffered under Pontius <u>Pi</u>late,
    was crucified, died <u>and</u> was buried;
* he descended into <u>hell</u>;
    on the third day he rose again <u>from</u> the dead;
* he ascended into <u>heav</u>en,
    and is seated at the right hand
       of God the Fa-<u>ther</u> almighty;
* from there he will <u>come</u>
    to judge the living <u>and</u> the dead.
* I believe in the Holy <u>Spir</u>it,
    the holy ca-<u>tho</u>lic Church,
* the communion of saints, the forgiveness of <u>sins</u>,
    the resurrection of the body,
       and life everlast-<u>ing</u>. Amen.

Text: *The Roman Missal,* © 2010, ICEL. All rights reserved.
Music: *Psallite Mass: At the Table of the Lord,* The Collegeville Composers Group, © 2010.
Published and administered by Liturgical Press, Collegeville, MN 56321. All rights reserved.

13. Apostles' Creed (Spanish)

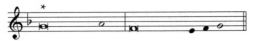

* Creo en Dios, Padre todopode-roso,
  Creador del cielo y de la tierra.
* Creo en Jesu-cristo,
  su único Hijo, nues-tro Señor,

En las palabras que siguen, hasta María Virgen, *todos se inclinan.*

* que fue concebido por obra y
      gracia del Espíritu Santo,
  nació de santa Ma-ría Virgen,
* padeció bajo el poder de Poncio Pi-lato,
  fue crucificado, muerto y sepultado,
* descendió a los in-fiernos,
  al tercer día resucitó de en-tre los muertos,
* subió a los cielos
  y está sentado a la derecha de Dios,
      Padre todo-poderoso.
* Desde allí ha de ve-nir
  a juzgar a vi-vos y muertos.
* Creo en el Espíritu Santo,
  la santa Iglesi-a católica,
* la comunión de los santos,
  el perdón de los pecados,
* la resurrección de la carne
  y la vida eter-na. Amén.

Text: *Misal Romano,* © 1999, 2002, Obra Nacional de la Buena Prensa, A.C. All rights reserved.
Music: *Psallite Mass: At the Table of the Lord,* The Collegeville Composers Group, © 2010.
Published and administered by Liturgical Press, Collegeville, MN 56321. All rights reserved.

14. Apostles' Creed (Latin)

* Credo in unum Deum
  Patrem omnipoténtem, Creatórem cæ-li et terræ,
* et in Iesum Christum,
  Fílium eius únicum, Dó-minum nostrum,

Ad verba quæ sequuntur, usque ad María Vírgine, *omnes se inclinant.*

* qui concéptus est de Spíritu Sancto,
  natus ex Ma-ría Vírgine,

* passus sub Póntio Pi-láto,
  crucifíxus, mórtuus, et sepúltus,
* descéndit ad ínferos,
  tértia die resurréx-it a mórtuis,
* ascéndit ad cælos,
  sedet ad déxteram Dei Patris om-nipoténtis,
* inde ven-túrus est
  iudicáre vi-vos et mórtuos.
* Credo in Spíritum Sanctum,
  sanctam Ecclési-am cathólicam,
* sanctórum communi-ónem,
  remissiónem peccatórum,
* carnis resurrecti-ónem,
  vitam ætér-nam. Amen.

Text: *Missale Romanum.*
Music: *Psallite Mass: At the Table of the Lord,* The Collegeville Composers Group, © 2010.
Published and administered by Liturgical Press, Collegeville, MN 56321. All rights reserved.

15. Sanctus (English, Spanish, Latin)

Holy, Holy, Holy Lord God of hosts.
Blessed is he who comes

Santo, Santo, Santo
es el Señor, Dios del U - ni - verso.
Bendito el que viene

Sanctus, Sanctus,
Sanctus Dóminus De - us Sábaoth.
Benedíc - tus qui venit

Heaven and earth are full of your glory.
in the name of the Lord.

Llenos están el cielo y la tierra de tu gloria.
en nombre del Se - ñor.

Pleni sunt cæli et terra gló - ri - a tua.
in nó - mi - ne Dómini.

Ho - san - na in the highest.
Ho - san - na in the highest.

Ho - san - na en el cielo.
Ho san - na en el cielo.

Ho - sán - na in ex - célsis.
Ho - sán - na in ex - célsis.

English text: *The Roman Missal,* © 2010, ICEL. All rights reserved.
Spanish text: *Misal Romano,* © 1999, 2002, Obra Nacional de la Buena Prensa, A.C.
All rights reserved.
Latin text: *Missale Romanum.*
Music: *Psallite Mass,* The Collegeville Composers Group, © 2010.
Published and administered by Liturgical Press, Collegeville, MN 56321. All rights reserved.

16. Mysterium Fidei – A (English, Spanish, Latin)

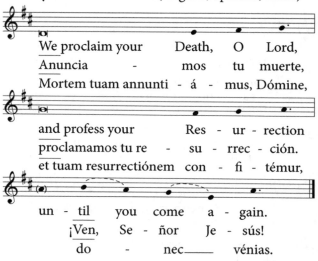

We proclaim your Death, O Lord,
Anuncia - mos tu muerte,
Mortem tuam annunti - á - mus, Dómine,

and profess your Res - ur - rection
proclamamos tu re - su - rrec - ción.
et tuam resurrectiónem con - fi - témur,

un - til you come a - gain.
¡Ven, Se - ñor Je - sús!
do - nec___ vénias.

17. Mysterium Fidei – B (English, Spanish, Latin)

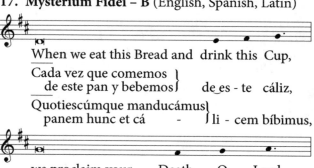

When we eat this Bread and drink this Cup,
Cada vez que comemos }
 de este pan y bebemos } de es - te cáliz,
Quotiescúmque manducámus }
 panem hunc et cá - } li - cem bíbimus,

we proclaim your Death, O Lord,
anunciamos tu muer - te, Se - ñor,
mortem tuam annunti - á - mus, Dómine,

un - til you come a - gain.
ha - sta que vuelvas.
do - nec_____ vénias.

18. Mysterium Fidei – C (English, Spanish, Latin)

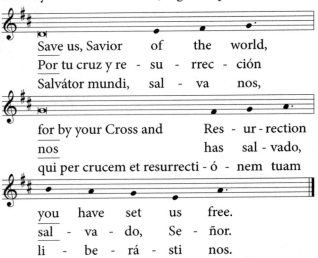

Save us, Savior of the world,
Por tu cruz y re - su - rrec - ción
Salvátor mundi, sal - va nos,

for by your Cross and Res - ur - rection
nos has sal - vado,
qui per crucem et resurrecti - ó - nem tuam

you have set us free.
sal - va - do, Se - ñor.
li - be - rá - sti nos.

19. Amen

A - men, A - men, A - men.

20. **Pater Noster** (English)

Our Father, who art in   heaven,   hallowed   be   thy   name;
thy kingdom come, thy will be   done   on earth as it   is   in   heaven.
Give us this day our daily   bread,   and forgive   us   our   trespasses,
as we forgive   those   who tres - pass   a - gainst us;
and lead us not into temp - tation,   but deliver   us   from   evil.

For the kingdom, the power
and the glory are   yours   now   and   for   ever.

Text: American edition of the *Book of Common Prayer*, 1790,
adapt. from the Anglican *Book of Common Prayer*, 1549.
Music: *Psallite Mass: At the Table of the Lord*, The Collegeville Composers Group, © 2010.
Published and administered by Liturgical Press, Collegeville, MN 56321. All rights reserved.

21. **Pater Noster** (Spanish)

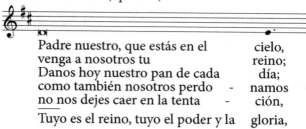

Padre nuestro, que estás en el   cielo,
venga a nosotros tu   reino;
Danos hoy nuestro pan de cada   día;
como también nosotros perdo - namos
no nos dejes caer en la tenta - ción,

Tuyo es el reino, tuyo el poder y la   gloria,

santificado   sea   tu   Nombre;
hágase tu voluntad ⎱
   en la tierra como ⎰   en   el   cielo.
perdona nue - stras   o - fensas,
a los que   nos   o - fenden;
y líbra - nos   del   mal.

por siem - pre,   Se - ñor.

22. Pater Noster (Latin)

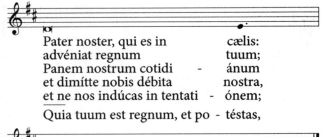

Pater noster, qui es in   cælis:
advéniat regnum   tuum;
Panem nostrum cotidi - ánum
et dimítte nobis débita   nostra,
et ne nos indúcas in tentati - ónem;

Quia tuum est regnum, et po - téstas,

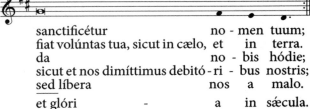

sanctificétur   no - men tuum;
fiat volúntas tua, sicut in cælo, et   in   terra.
da   no - bis hódie;
sicut et nos dimíttimus debitó - ri - bus nostris;
sed líbera   nos   a   malo.

et glóri - a   in   sǽcula.

23. Agnus Dei (English, Spanish, Latin)

Cantor:

Choir and/or assembly:

A - gnus Dei,   qui tollis peccáta
Lamb of God,   you take away the sins of the
Cordero de Dios,   que quitas el pecado del
A - gnus Dei,   qui tollis peccáta

All: (To repeat)

mundi: mi - se - ré - re no - bis.
world:
mundo:
mundi:

All: (Last time)

do - na no - bis pa - cem.

Spanish text: *Misal Romano*, © 1999, 2002, Obra Nacional de la Buena Prensa, A.C.
All rights reserved.
Music: *Psallite Mass*, The Collegeville Composers Group, © 2010.
Published and administered by Liturgical Press, Collegeville, MN 56321. All rights reserved.

Mass II—Missa Iubilate Deo

the Vatican Edition

24. Kyrie

Repeat each phrase after the Priest, Deacon, or Cantor

Ký-ri - e, e-lé-i-son. Chri-ste, e-lé-i-son.

Optional final ending by all

Ký-ri - e, e-lé-i-son. Ký-ri - e, e-lé - i-son.

Text and music: Mass XVI, Mode III, from *Cantus Missae*, Vatican ed., 1974.

25. Gloria

Gló-ri-a in ex-cél-sis De-o et in ter-ra

pax ho-mí-ni-bus bo-næ vo-lun-tá-tis.

Lau-dá-mus te, be-ne-dí-ci-mus te,

a-do-rá-mus te, glo-ri-fi-cá-mus te,

grá-ti-as á-gi-mus ti - bi pro-pter ma-

gnam gló-ri-am tu-am, Dó-mi-ne De-us,

Rex cæ-lé-stis, De-us Pa-ter o-mní-po-tens.

Dó-mi-ne Fi-li U-ni-gé-ni-te, Ie-su Chri-ste, Dó-mi-ne De-us, A-gnus De-i, Fí-li-us Pa-tris, qui tol-lis pec-cá-ta mun-di, mi-se-ré-re no-bis; qui tol-lis pec-cá-ta mun-di, sú-sci-pe de-pre-ca-ti-ó-nem no-stram. Qui se-des ad déx-te-ram Pa-tris, mi-se-ré-re no-bis. Quó-ni-am tu so-lus San-ctus, tu so-lus Dó-mi-nus, tu so-lus Al-tís-si-mus, Ie-su Chri-ste, cum San-cto Spí-ri-tu: in gló-ri-a De-i Pa-tris. A-men.

Text and music: Mass VIII, Mode V, from *Cantus Missae*, Vatican ed., 1974.

26. Ad Liturgiam Verbi

Response I to Reading *when two readings precede gospel*

Reader/Cantor: Verbum Dó - mi - ni.
All: Deo grá - ti - as.

Response II to Reading *or when one reading precedes gospel*

Reader/Cantor: Verbum Dó - mi - ni.
All: Deo grá - ti - as.

Gospel Acclamation

Cantor/All: Al - le - lú - ia, al - le - lú - ia, al - le - lú - ia.

Introduction to the Gospel

Deacon/Priest: Dóminus vobís - cum.
All: Et cum spíritu tu - o.

Deacon/Priest: Léctio sancti Evangélii secún - dum N.

All: Glória ti - bi, Dó - mi - ne.

Conclusion to the Gospel

Deacon/Priest: Verbum Dó - mi - ni.
All: Laus tibi, Chri - ste.

Text and music: *Cantus Missae,* Vatican ed., 1974.

27. Credo

Priest/Cantor: Cre-do in u-num De - um, *All:* Pa-trem o-mni-po-tén-tem, fa-ctó-rem cæ-li et ter-ræ, vi-si-bí-li-um ó - mni-um et in-vi-si-bí - li-um. Et in u-num Dó-mi-num Ie-sum Chri-stum, Fí-li-um De-i U-ni-gé-ni-tum, et ex Pa-tre na - tum an-te ó-mni-a sǽ - cu-la. De-um de De-o, lu-men de lú-mi-ne, De-um ve-rum de De-o ve-ro, gé-ni-tum, non fa - ctum, con-sub-stan-ti - á-lem Pa-tri: per quem ó-mni-a fa-cta sunt. Qui pro-pter nos hó-mi-nes et pro-pter

no-stram sa-lú-tem de-scén-dit de cæ-lis.

Ad verba quæ sequuntur, usque ad factus est, *omnes se inclinant.*

Et in-car-ná-tus est de Spí-ri-tu San-cto

ex Ma-rí-a Vír-gi-ne, et ho-mo fa-ctus est.

Cru-ci - fí - xus é-ti-am pro no-bis

sub Pón-ti-o Pi-lá-to; pas-sus et se-púl-

tus est, et re-sur-ré-xit tér-ti-a di-e,

se-cún-dum Scrip-tú-ras, et a-scén-dit

in cæ-lum, se-det ad déx-te-ram Pa - tris.

Et í-te-rum ven-tú-rus est cum gló-ri-a,

iu-di-cá-re vi-vos et mór-tu-os, cu-ius re-gni

non e-rit fí-nis. Et in Spí-ri-tum San-ctum,

Dó-mi-num et vi-vi-fi-cán-tem: qui ex Pa-tre Fi-li-ó-que pro-cé-dit. Qui cum Pa-tre et Fí-li-o si-mul a-do-rá-tur et con-glo-ri-fi-cá-tur: qui lo-cú-tus est per pro-phé-tas. Et u-nam, san-ctam, ca-thó-li-cam et a-po-stó-li-cam Ec-clé-si-am. Con-fí-te-or u-num bap-tís-ma in re-mis-si-ó-nem pec-ca-tó-rum. Et ex-spé-cto re-sur-re-cti-ó-nem mor-tu-ó-rum, et vi-tam ven-tú-ri sǽ-cu-li. A - men.

Text and music: *Cantus Missae*, Vatican ed., 1974.

28. Ad Orationem Universalem

Deacon or Cantor:

. . . ex-au-di-re di-gné - ris.

All:

Te ro-gá-mus, au-di nos.

Text and music: *Cantus Missae*, Vatican ed., 1974.

29. Ante Praefationem

Priest: *All:*

Dó-mi-nus vo-bís-cum. Et cum spí-ri-tu tu-o.

Priest: *All:*

Sur-sum cor-da. Ha-bé-mus ad Dó-mi-num.

Priest:

Grá-ti-as a-gá-mus Dó-mi-no De-o no-stro.

All:

Di - gnum et iu-stum est.

Text and music: *Cantus Missae*, Vatican ed., 1974.

30. Sanctus

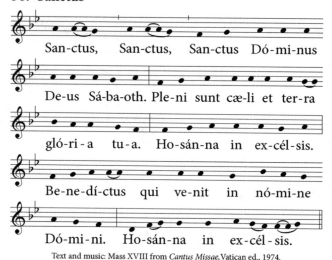

San-ctus, San-ctus, San-ctus Dó-mi-nus
De-us Sá-ba-oth. Ple-ni sunt cæ-li et ter-ra
gló-ri-a tu-a. Ho-sán-na in ex-cél-sis.
Be-ne-dí-ctus qui ve-nit in nó-mi-ne
Dó-mi-ni. Ho-sán-na in ex-cél-sis.

Text and music: Mass XVIII from *Cantus Missae*, Vatican ed., 1974.

31. Mysterium Fidei

Priest: Or

My-sté-ri-um fí-de-i. My-sté-ri-um fí-de-i.

All:

Mor-tem tu-am an-nun-ti-á-mus,
Dó-mi-ne, et tu-am re-sur-rec-ti-ó-nem
con-fi-té-mur, do-nec vé-ni-as.

Text and music: *Cantus Missae*, Vatican ed., 1974.

32. Amen

Priest: . . . sǽ-cu-la sæ-cu-ló-rum. All: A - men.

Text and music: *Cantus Missae*, Vatican ed., 1974.

33. Pater Noster

All:
Pa-ter no-ster, qui es in cæ-lis: san-cti-fi-

cé-tur no-men tu-um; ad-vé-ni-at re-gnum

tu-um; fi-at vo-lún-tas tu-a, si-cut in cæ-lo,

et in ter-ra. Pa-nem no-strum co-ti-di-

á-num da no-bis hó-di-e; et di-mít-te no-bis

dé-bi-ta no-stra, si-cut et nos di-mít-ti-mus

de-bi-tó-ri-bus no-stris; et ne nos in-dú-cas in

ten-ta-ti-ó-nem; sed lí-be-ra nos a ma-lo.

Priest: *Líbera nos, quǽsumus . . . nostri Iesu Christi.*

All:

Qui - a tu - um est re - gnum, et po - té - stas, et gló - ri - a in sǽ-cu-la.

Text and music: *Cantus Missae,* Vatican ed., 1974.

34. Agnus Dei

A - gnus De - i, qui tol - lis pec - cá - ta mun - di, mi - se - ré - re no - bis.

A - gnus De - i, qui tol - lis pec - cá - ta mun - di, mi - se - ré - re no - bis.

A - gnus De - i, qui tol - lis pec - cá - ta mun - di, do - na no - bis pa - cem.

Text and music: *Cantus Missae,* Vatican ed., 1974.

35. Ad Ritus Conclusionis

Blessing

Dóminus vobís - cum. Et cum spíritu tu - o.

Benedícat vos omní - po - tens De - us,

Pa - ter, et Fílius, et Spíritus San - ctus. A - men.

Dismissal I – Outside the Easter season

I - te, mis - sa est. De - o grá - ti - as.

Dismissal II – During the Easter season

Deacon/Priest sings "Ite missa est . . ." to which the people respond "Deo gratias . . ."

I - te, mis - sa est, al - le - lú - ia,
De - o grá - ti - as, al - le - lú - ia,

al - le - lú - ia.
al - le - lú - ia.

Text and music: *Cantus Missae*, Vatican ed., 1974.

Mass III—in Honor of Saint Benedict

by Robert LeBlanc

36. Kyrie

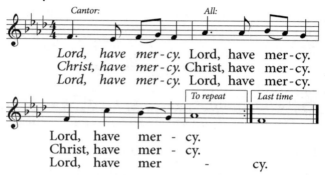

Lord, have mer-cy. Lord, have mer-cy.
Christ, have mer-cy. Christ, have mer-cy.
Lord, have mer-cy. Lord, have mer-cy.

Lord, have mer - cy.
Christ, have mer - cy.
Lord, have mer - cy.

Music: *Mass in Honor of Saint Benedict*, Robert LeBlanc, © 1991.
Published and administered by Liturgical Press, Collegeville, MN 56321. All rights reserved.

37. Gloria

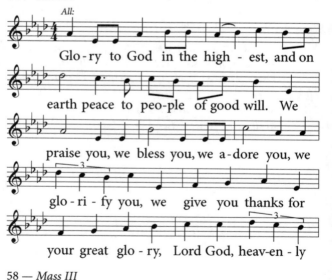

Glo-ry to God in the high - est, and on
earth peace to peo-ple of good will. We
praise you, we bless you, we a-dore you, we
glo-ri-fy you, we give you thanks for
your great glo-ry, Lord God, heav-en-ly

King, O God, al-might-y Fa-ther.

Cantor/Choir or All:

Lord Je-sus Christ, On-ly Be-got-ten

Son, Lord God, Lamb of God,

Son of the Fa-ther, you take a-way the

sins of the world, have mer-cy on us;

you take a-way the sins of the world,

re-ceive our prayer; you are

seat-ed at the right hand of the

Fa-ther, have mer-cy on us.

All:

For you a-lone are the Ho-ly One,

you a-lone are the Lord,

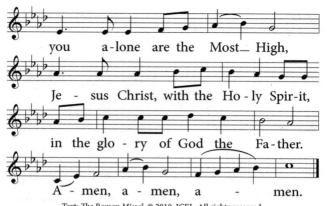

you a-lone are the Most High, Je-sus Christ, with the Ho-ly Spir-it, in the glo-ry of God the Fa-ther. A-men, a-men, a-men.

38. Gospel Acclamation

Al-le-lu-ia, al-le-lu-ia, al-le-lu-ia.

39. Gospel Acclamation (Lent)

Glo-ry and praise to you, Lord Je-sus Christ!

40. Sanctus

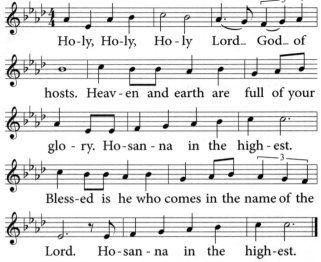

Ho-ly, Ho-ly, Ho-ly Lord_ God_ of hosts. Heav-en and earth are full of your glo-ry. Ho-san-na in the high-est. Bless-ed is he who comes in the name of the Lord. Ho-san-na in the high-est.

Text: *The Roman Missal*, © 2010, ICEL. All rights reserved.
Music: *Mass in Honor of Saint Benedict*, Robert LeBlanc, © 1991, 2010.
Published and administered by Liturgical Press, Collegeville, MN 56321. All rights reserved.

41. Mysterium Fidei – A

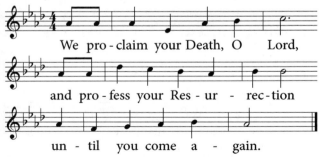

We pro-claim your Death, O Lord, and pro-fess your Res-ur - rec-tion un - til you come a - gain.

42. Mysterium Fidei – B

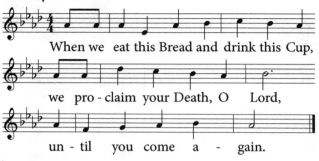

When we eat this Bread and drink this Cup,

we pro - claim your Death, O Lord,

un - til you come a - gain.

43. Mysterium Fidei – C

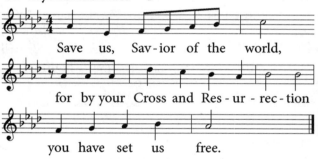

Save us, Sav-ior of the world,

for by your Cross and Res - ur - rec - tion

you have set us free.

Text: *The Roman Missal,* © 2010, ICEL. All rights reserved.
Music: *Mass in Honor of Saint Benedict,* Robert LeBlanc, © 2010.
Published and administered by Liturgical Press, Collegeville, MN 56321. All rights reserved.

44. Amen

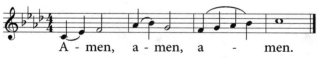

A - men, a - men, a - men.

Music: *Mass in Honor of Saint Benedict,* Robert LeBlanc, © 1991.
Published and administered by Liturgical Press, Collegeville, MN 56321. All rights reserved.

45. Agnus Dei

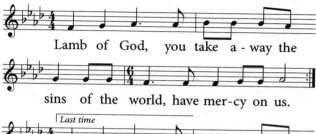

Lamb of God, you take a - way the sins of the world, have mer-cy on us.

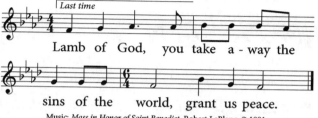

Last time

Lamb of God, you take a - way the sins of the world, grant us peace.

Music: *Mass in Honor of Saint Benedict,* Robert LeBlanc, © 1991.
Published and administered by Liturgical Press, Collegeville, MN 56321. All rights reserved.

Mass IV—in A Minor

by Frederick W. Strassburger

46. Kyrie

Priest, Deacon, or Cantor: Lord,— have mer-cy. *All:* Lord,— have mer-cy.

Priest, Deacon, or Cantor: Christ,— have mer-cy. *All:* Christ,— have mer-cy.

Priest, Deacon, or Cantor: Lord,— have mer-cy. *All:* Lord,— have mer-cy.

Music: *Mass in A Minor*, Frederick W. Strassburger, © 2010.
Published and administered by Liturgical Press, Collegeville, MN 56321. All rights reserved.

47. Gloria

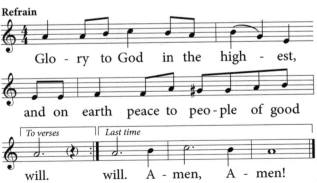

Refrain

Glo-ry to God in the high - est, and on earth peace to peo-ple of good will. *To verses* will. *Last time* A - men, A - men!

Verse 1

We praise you, we bless you, we a - dore you, we glo - ri - fy you, we give you thanks for your great glo - ry, Lord God, heav - en - ly King, O God, al - might - y Fa - ther. *D.C.*

Verse 2

Lord Je - sus Christ, On - ly Be - got - ten Son, Lord God, Lamb of God, Son of the Fa - ther, you take a - way the sins of the world, have mer - cy on us; you take a - way the sins of the world, re - ceive our prayer; you are seat - ed at the right hand of the Fa - ther, have mer - cy on us. *D.C.*

Verse 3

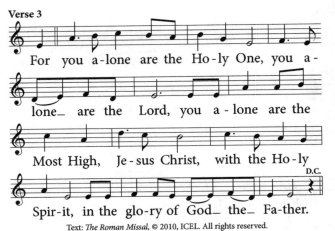

For you a-lone are the Ho-ly One, you a-lone_ are the Lord, you a-lone are the Most High, Je-sus Christ, with the Ho-ly Spir-it, in the glo-ry of God_ the_ Fa-ther.

48. Gospel Acclamation

Al - le-lu - ia, al - le-lu - ia, al - le-lu - ia!

49. Gospel Acclamation (Lent)

Praise to you,— Lord Je - sus Christ,
King of end - less— glo - ry!

50. Sanctus

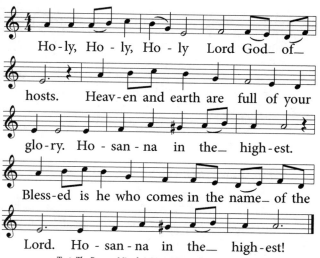

Ho - ly, Ho - ly, Ho - ly Lord God— of—
hosts. Heav - en and earth are full of your
glo - ry. Ho - san - na in the— high - est.
Bless - ed is he who comes in the name— of the
Lord. Ho - san - na in the— high - est!

51. Mysterium Fidei – A

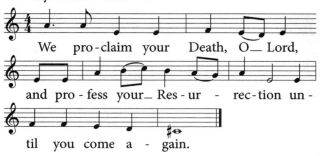

We pro-claim your Death, O— Lord,
and pro-fess your Res-ur - rec-tion un-
til you come a - gain.

52. Mysterium Fidei – B

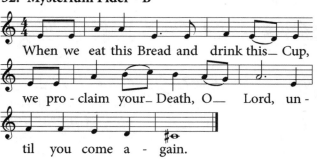

When we eat this Bread and drink this— Cup,
we pro - claim your— Death, O— Lord, un -
til you come a - gain.

53. Mysterium Fidei – C

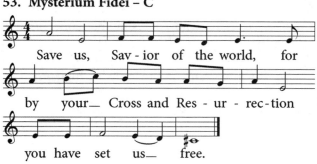

Save us, Sav - ior of the world, for
by your— Cross and Res - ur - rec-tion
you have set us— free.

54. Amen

A - men, a - men, a - men.

Music: *Mass in A Minor,* Frederick W. Strassburger, © 2010.
Published and administered by Liturgical Press, Collegeville, MN 56321. All rights reserved.

55. Agnus Dei

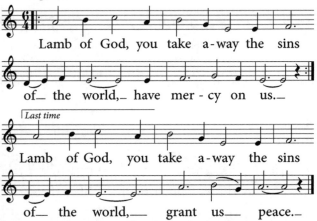

Lamb of God, you take a-way the sins

of_ the world,_ have mer - cy on us._

Last time

Lamb of God, you take a-way the sins

of_ the world,_ grant us_ peace._

Music: *Mass in A Minor,* Frederick W. Strassburger, © 2010.
Published and administered by Liturgical Press, Collegeville, MN 56321. All rights reserved.

Mass V—in Honor of Mary, Mother of God

by Donald Krubsack

56. Kyrie

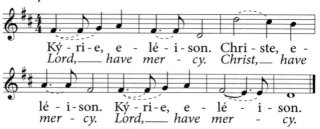

Ký - ri - e, e - lé - i - son. Chri - ste, e -
Lord,— have mer - cy. Christ,— have

lé - i - son. Ký - ri - e, e - lé - i - son.
mer - cy. Lord,— have mer - cy.

57. Gloria

Refrain

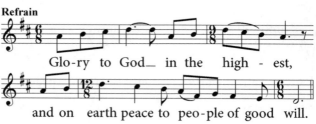

Glo - ry to God— in the high - est,

and on earth peace to peo - ple of good will.

Verse 1

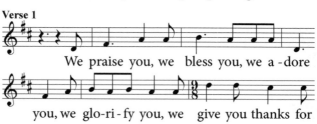

We praise you, we bless you, we a - dore

you, we glo - ri - fy you, we give you thanks for

your great glory, Lord God, hea-ven-ly

To refrain

King, O God, al-might-y Fa-ther.

Verse 2

Lord Je-sus Christ, On-ly Be-got-ten

Son, Lord God, Lamb of God, Son of the

Fa-ther, you take a-way the sins of the

world, have mer-cy on us; you

take a-way the sins of the world,

re-ceive our prayer; you are seat-ed

at the right hand of the Fa-ther,

To refrain

have mer-cy on us.

Verse 3

For you a-lone are the Ho-ly One, you a-lone are the Lord, you a-lone are the Most High, Je-sus Christ, with the Ho-ly Spir- *To final refrain* it, in the glo-ry of God the Fa-ther.

Final Refrain

Glo-ry to God in the high-est, and on earth peace to peo-ple of good will. A-men. A-men.

58. Gospel Acclamation

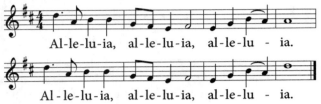

Al-le-lu-ia, al-le-lu-ia, al-le-lu - ia.

Al-le-lu-ia, al-le-lu-ia, al-le-lu - ia.

59. Gospel Acclamation (Lent)

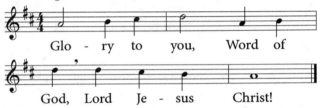

Glo - ry to you, Word of

God, Lord Je - sus Christ!

60. Gospel Acclamation (Lent)

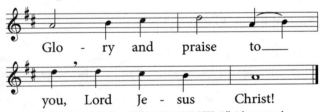

Glo - ry and praise to___

you, Lord Je - sus Christ!

61. Sanctus

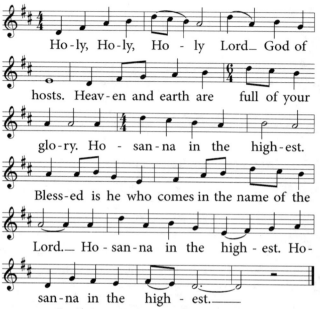

Ho-ly, Ho-ly, Ho - ly Lord_ God of hosts. Heav-en and earth are full of your glo-ry. Ho - san-na in the high-est. Bless-ed is he who comes in the name of the Lord._ Ho - san-na in the high - est. Ho-san-na in the high - est._

62. Mysterium Fidei

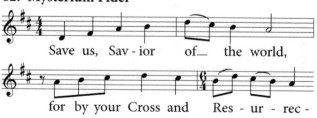

Save us, Sav - ior of_ the world, for by your Cross and Res - ur - rec-

tion   you have set us   free.

63. Amen

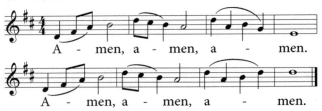

A - men, a - men, a - men.

A - men, a - men, a - men.

64. Agnus Dei

Cantor/choir: *All:*

Lamb of God, you take a - way the

sins of the world, have mer-cy on

us. world,

grant us peace.

Mass VI—in Honor of Saint Cloud

by Jay F. Hunstiger

65. Kyrie

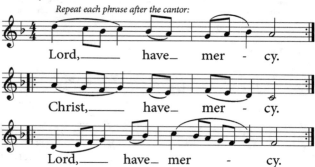

Repeat each phrase after the cantor:

Lord,_____ have_ mer - cy.

Christ,_____ have_ mer - cy.

Lord,_____ have_ mer - cy.

66. Gloria

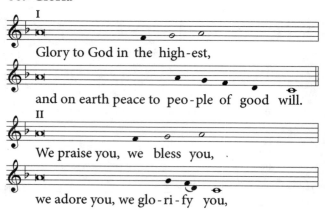

I

Glory to God in the high-est,

and on earth peace to peo-ple of good will.

II

We praise you, we bless you,

we adore you, we glo-ri-fy you,

we give you thanks for your great glo-ry,

Lord God, heavenly King, O God, al-might-y Father.

Lord Jesus Christ, Only Begot-ten Son,

Lord God, Lamb of God, Son of the Father,

you take away the sins of the world,

have mer-cy on us;

you take away the sins of the world,

re-ceive our prayer;

you are seated at the right hand of the Fa-ther,

have mer-cy on us._____

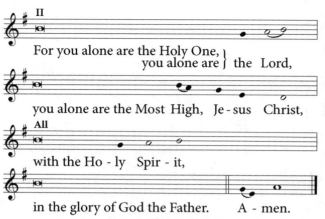

For you alone are the Holy One,
you alone are the Lord,

you alone are the Most High, Je-sus Christ,

All

with the Ho-ly Spir-it,

in the glory of God the Father.   A - men.

67. Gospel Acclamation

Al-le - lu – ia,   al-le - lu - ia,—

al-le - lu – ia.

68. Gospel Acclamation (Lent)

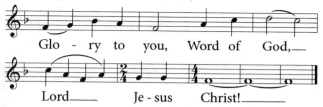

Glo - ry to you, Word of God,— Lord— Je - sus Christ!—

69. Sanctus

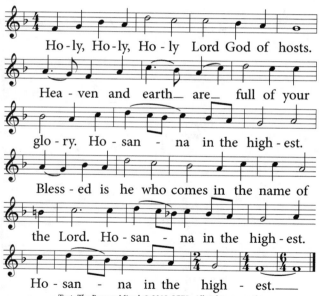

Ho - ly, Ho - ly, Ho - ly Lord God of hosts.
Hea - ven and earth— are— full of your
glo - ry. Ho - san - na in the high - est.
Bless - ed is he who comes in the name of
the Lord. Ho - san - na in the high - est.
Ho - san - na in the high - est.—

70. Mysterium Fidei

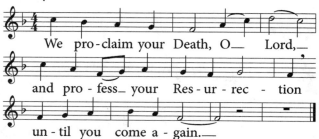

We pro-claim your Death, O— Lord,— and pro-fess— your Res-ur-rec-tion un-til you come a-gain.—

71. Amen

A - men, a - men,— a - men.

72. Agnus Dei

Cantor: *All:* Lamb of God, you take a-way the— sins— of the

To repeat
world, have mer-cy on—— us.

Last time
world, grant us peace.

Mass VII—in Honor of Saint Michael

by Kevin Christopher Vogt

73. Kyrie

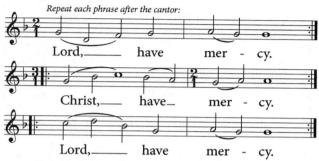

Repeat each phrase after the cantor:

Lord, have mer - cy.

Christ, have mer - cy.

Lord, have mer - cy.

74. Gloria

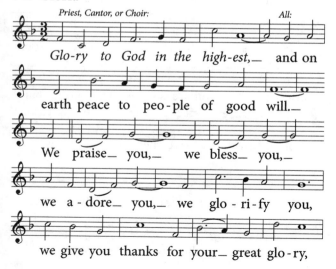

Priest, Cantor, or Choir: All:

Glo-ry to God in the high-est,— and on

earth peace to peo-ple of good will.—

We praise— you,— we bless— you,—

we a-dore— you,— we glo-ri-fy you,

we give you thanks for your— great glo-ry,

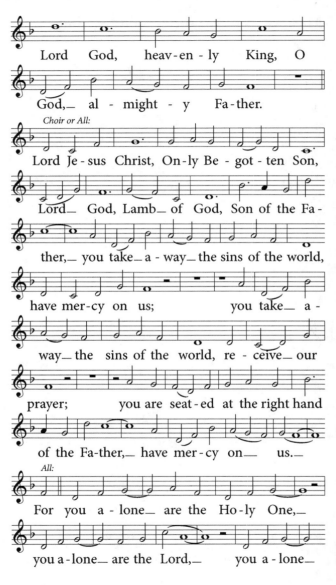

Lord God, heav-en-ly King, O

God,— al - might - y Fa-ther.

Choir or All:

Lord Je - sus Christ, On-ly Be - got - ten Son,

Lord— God, Lamb— of God, Son of the Fa-

ther,— you take— a - way— the sins of the world,

have mer-cy on us; you take— a -

way— the sins of the world, re - ceive— our

prayer; you are seat-ed at the right hand

of the Fa-ther,— have mer-cy on— us.—

All:

For you a - lone— are the Ho-ly One,—

you a-lone— are the Lord,— you a-lone—

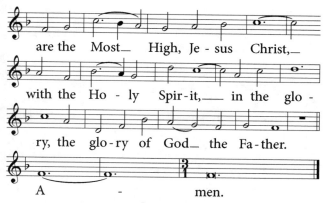

are the Most High, Je-sus Christ,

with the Ho-ly Spir-it, in the glo-

ry, the glo-ry of God the Fa-ther.

A — men.

75. Gospel Acclamation

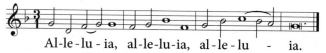

Al-le-lu-ia, al-le-lu-ia, al-le-lu - ia.

76. Gospel Acclamation (Lent)

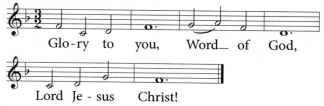

Glo-ry to you, Word of God,

Lord Je-sus Christ!

77. Sanctus

Ho - ly, Ho - ly, Ho - ly Lord— God of hosts. Heav-en and earth are full of your glo-ry.— Ho - san - na in— the high-est. Bless-ed is he— who comes in the name of the Lord.—— Ho - san - na, ho - san - na in— the high-est.

78. Mysterium Fidei – A

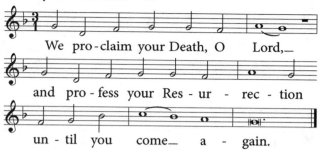

We pro-claim your Death, O Lord,—
and pro-fess your Res - ur - rec - tion
un - til you come— a - gain.

79. Mysterium Fidei – B

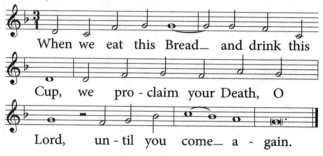

When we eat this Bread— and drink this
Cup, we pro - claim your Death, O
Lord, un - til you come— a - gain.

80. Mysterium Fidei – C

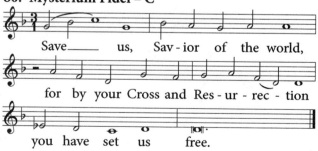

Save——— us, Sav - ior of the world,
for by your Cross and Res - ur - rec - tion
you have set us free.

Text: *The Roman Missal*, © 2010, ICEL. All rights reserved.
Music: *Mass in Honor of Saint Michael*, Kevin Christopher Vogt, © 2010.
Published and administered by Liturgical Press, Collegeville, MN 56321. All rights reserved.

81. Amen

A - men, a - men, a - men.

82. Agnus Dei

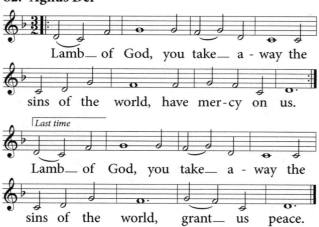

Lamb— of God, you take— a - way the sins of the world, have mer-cy on us.

Last time

Lamb— of God, you take— a - way the sins of the world, grant— us peace.

Mass VIII—an Austrian Mass

by Michael Haydn, arranged by Anthony Ruff, OSB

83. Sanctus

Ho-ly, Ho-ly, Ho-ly Lord God___ of hosts. Hea-ven and earth___ are full___ of___ your___ glo-ry. Ho-san-na in the high-est, ho-san-na___ in the high-est. Bless-ed is he___ who comes in the name___ of the Lord.___ Ho-san-na in the high-est, ho-san-na___ in the high-est, ho-san-na in the high-est.

Text: *The Roman Missal*, © 2010, ICEL. All rights reserved.
Music: *Singmesse* by Michael Haydn, 1795, adapt. by Anthony Ruff, OSB, © 2010.
Published and administered by Liturgical Press, Collegeville, MN 56321. All rights reserved.

84. Mysterium Fidei – A

We pro-claim your Death, O Lord, and pro-fess your Res-ur-rec-tion un-til you come a-gain.

85. Mysterium Fidei – B

When we eat this Bread and drink this Cup, we pro-claim your Death, O Lord, un-til you come a-gain.

86. Mysterium Fidei – C

Save us, Sav-ior of the world, for by your Cross and Res-ur-rec-tion you have set us free.

Text: *The Roman Missal,* © 2010, ICEL. All rights reserved.
Music: *Singmesse* by Michael Haydn, 1795, adapt. by Anthony Ruff, OSB, © 2010.
Published and administered by Liturgical Press, Collegeville, MN 56321. All rights reserved.

87. Amen

A - men, a - men, a - men,___ a - men.

Music: *Singmesse* by Michael Haydn, 1795, adapt. by Anthony Ruff, OSB, © 2010.

88. Agnus Dei

Lamb___ of God, you___ take a - way___ the
sins of the world, have mer - cy on us.
Lamb___ of God, you take___ a - way___ the
sins of the world, have mer-cy on us.___
Lamb___ of God, you___ take a - way___ the
sins of the world,___ grant us peace,
grant___ us peace,___ grant us peace.

Music: *Singmesse* by Michael Haydn, 1795, adapt. by Anthony Ruff, OSB, © 2010.

Mass IX—in Honor of Saint Cecilia

by David Hurd

89. Kyrie

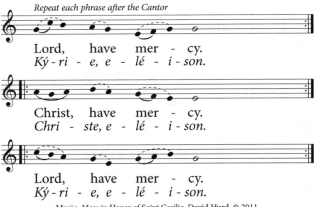

Repeat each phrase after the Cantor

Lord, have mer - cy.
Ký - ri - e, e - lé - i - son.

Christ, have mer - cy.
Chri - ste, e - lé - i - son.

Lord, have mer - cy.
Ký - ri - e, e - lé - i - son.

90. Gloria

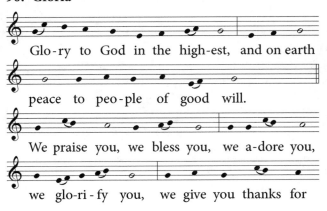

Glo-ry to God in the high-est, and on earth

peace to peo-ple of good will.

We praise you, we bless you, we a-dore you,

we glo-ri - fy you, we give you thanks for

your great glo-ry, Lord God, heav-en-ly
King, O God, al-might-y Fa-ther.
Lord Je-sus Christ, On-ly Be-got-ten Son,
Lord God, Lamb of God, Son of the Fa-ther,
you take a-way the sins of the world,
have mer-cy on us; you take a-way the
sins of the world, re-ceive our prayer;
you are seat-ed at the right hand of the Fa-ther,
have mer-cy on us. For you a-lone are the
Ho-ly One, you a-lone are the Lord,
you a-lone are the Most High, Je-sus Christ,

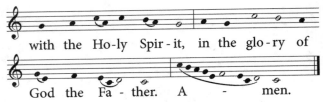

with the Ho-ly Spir-it, in the glo-ry of God the Fa-ther. A - men.

91. Gospel Acclamation

Al-le-lu-ia, al-le-lu-ia, al-le-lu - ia.

92. Gospel Acclamation (Lent)

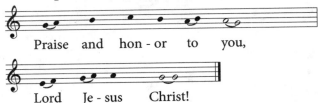

Praise and hon-or to you, Lord Je-sus Christ!

93. Credo

I be-lieve in one God, the Fa-ther al-

might-y, ma-ker of heav-en and earth,

of all things vi-si-ble and in-vi-si-ble.

I be-lieve in one Lord Je-sus Christ,

the On-ly Be-got-ten Son of God,

born of the Fa-ther be-fore all a-ges.

God from God, Light from Light, true

God from true God, be-got-ten, not made,

con-sub-stan-tial with the Fa-ther;

through him all things were made.

For us men and for our sal-va-tion

he came down from heav-en,

All bow from here through the words and became man.

and by the Ho-ly Spir-it was in-car-nate of the Vir-gin Mar-y, and be-came man.

For our sake he was cru-ci-fied un-der Pon-tius Pi-late, he suf-fered death and was bur-ied, and rose a-gain on the third day in ac-cor-dance with the Scrip-tures. He as-cend-ed in-to heav-en and is seat-ed at the right hand of the Fa-ther. He will come a-gain in glo-ry to judge the liv-ing and the dead and his king-dom will have no end.

I believe in the Holy Spirit, the Lord, the giver of life, who proceeds from the Father and the Son, who with the Father and the Son is adored and glorified, who has spoken through the prophets. I believe in one, holy, catholic and apostolic Church. I confess one Baptism for the forgiveness of sins and I look forward to the resurrection of the dead and the life of the world to come. A - men.

94. Sanctus

Ho - ly, Ho - ly, Ho - ly Lord
God of hosts. Heav-en and earth are
full of your glo-ry. Ho-san - na
in the high-est. Bless-ed is he
who comes in the name of the Lord.
Ho-san - na in the high-est.

Text: *The Roman Missal,* © 2010, ICEL. All rights reserved.
Music: *Mass in Honor of Saint Cecilia,* David Hurd, © 2011.
Published and administered by Liturgical Press, Collegeville, MN 56321. All rights reserved.

95. Mysterium Fidei – A

We pro-claim your Death, O Lord,

and pro-fess your Res-ur-rec-tion

un-til you come a-gain.

96. Mysterium Fidei – B

When we eat this Bread and drink this Cup,

we pro-claim your Death, O Lord,

un-til you come a-gain.

97. Mysterium Fidei – C

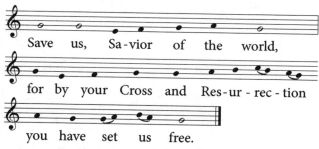

Save us, Sa-vior of the world,

for by your Cross and Res-ur-rec-tion

you have set us free.

Text: *The Roman Missal,* © 2010, ICEL. All rights reserved.
Music: *Mass in Honor of Saint Cecilia,* David Hurd, © 2011.
Published and administered by Liturgical Press, Collegeville, MN 56321. All rights reserved.

98. Amen

A - men, a - men, a - men.

99. Agnus Dei

Lamb of God, you take a-way the sins of the world, have mer-cy on us.

Lamb of God, you take a-way the sins of the world, have mer-cy on us.

Lamb of God, you take a-way the sins of the world, grant us peace.

Mass X—in Honor of Saint Dominic

by Matthew S. Still

100. Kyrie

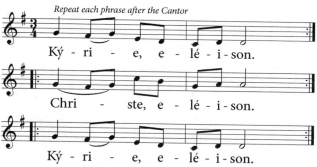

Repeat each phrase after the Cantor

Ký - ri - e, e - lé - i - son.

Chri - ste, e - lé - i - son.

Ký - ri - e, e - lé - i - son.

101. Gloria

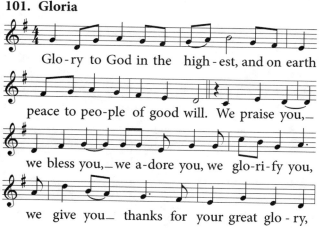

Glo - ry to God in the high - est, and on earth

peace to peo - ple of good will. We praise you,

we bless you,— we a - dore you, we glo - ri - fy you,

we give you— thanks for your great glo - ry,

Lord God, heav-en-ly King, O God, al-might-y Fa-ther.— Lord Je-sus Christ, On-ly Be-got-ten Son, Lord— God, Lamb of God, Son of the Fa-ther,— you take a-way the sins of the world, have mer-cy on us; you take a-way the sins of the world, re-ceive— our prayer; you are— seat-ed at the right hand of the Fa-ther, have mer-cy on us. For you a-lone are the Ho-ly One, you a-lone are the Lord,— you a-lone are the

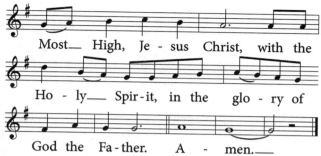

Most— High, Je-sus Christ, with the Ho-ly— Spir-it, in the glo-ry of God the Fa-ther. A— men.—

102. Gospel Acclamation

Al-le-lu-ia, al-le-lu-ia, al-le-lu-ia.

103. Gospel Acclamation (Lent)

Praise to you, Lord Je-sus Christ, King of end-less glo-ry!

104. Sanctus

Ho-ly, Ho-ly, Ho-ly Lord God of hosts. Heav-en and earth are full of your glo-ry. Ho-san-na, ho-san-na, ho-san-na in the high-est. Bless-ed is he who comes in the name of the Lord. Ho-san-na, ho-san-na, ho-san-na in the high-est. Ho-san-na, ho-san-na, ho-san-na in the high-est.

Text: *The Roman Missal*, © 2010, ICEL. All rights reserved.
Music: *Mass in Honor of Saint Dominic*, Matthew S. Still, © 2011.
Published and administered by Liturgical Press, Collegeville, MN 56321. All rights reserved.

105. Mysterium Fidei – A

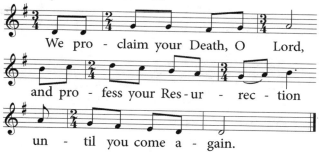

We pro - claim your Death, O Lord, and pro - fess your Res - ur - rec - tion un - til you come a - gain.

106. Mysterium Fidei – B

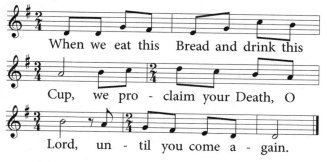

When we eat this Bread and drink this Cup, we pro - claim your Death, O Lord, un - til you come a - gain.

107. Mysterium Fidei – C

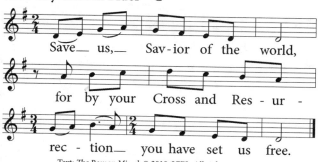

Save us, Sav-ior of the world, for by your Cross and Res - ur - rec - tion you have set us free.

Text: *The Roman Missal*, © 2010, ICEL. All rights reserved.
Music: *Mass in Honor of Saint Dominic*, Matthew S. Still, © 2011.
Published and administered by Liturgical Press, Collegeville, MN 56321. All rights reserved.

108. Amen

A - men, — a - men, a - men. —

109. Agnus Dei

Cantor: All:

Lamb — of God, — you take a - way the

To repeat

sins — of the world, have mer-cy on us.

Last time

sins — of the world, grant —

us peace. —